TORNADO

Wick Poetry Chapbook Series Four
Maggie Anderson, Editor

How to Paint the Savior Dead
Jason Gray

The Space Between Stars
Matt McBride

Spotlit Girl
Kevin Oberlin

Tornado
Ted Lardner

TORNADO

Poems by Ted Lardner

The Kent State University Press
Kent, Ohio

Ohio Arts Council
A STATE AGENCY
THAT SUPPORTS PUBLIC
PROGRAMS IN THE ARTS

Library of Congress Catalog Card Number 2007047309
ISBN 978-0-87338-955-6
Manufactured in the United States of America

The Wick Poetry Series is sponsored in part by the
Wick Poetry Center at Kent State University.

Library of Congress Cataloging-in-Publication Data
Lardner, Ted.
    Tornado : poems / by Ted Lardner.
            p. cm. — (Wick poetry chapbook series four)
    ISBN 978-0-87338-955-6 (pbk. : alk. paper)∞
    I. Title.
PS3612.A648T67   2008
811'.6—dc22   2007047309

British Library Cataloging-in-Publication data are available.

12 11 10 09 08   5 4 3 2 1

for
H. E. L.

CONTENTS

ACKNOWLEDGMENTS

Thanks to the editors of these magazines for publishing, sometimes in different versions, the following poems: "Eye," "X," *5am*; "I Look at the Apple Tree," "Bath," *Clackamas Literary Review*; "From Afar," "Singing," *Rhino*; "Poem for a Son," *Arsenic Lobster*; "Lullaby," *Pleiades*; "Memorial for My Life," *Crab Creek Review*. Foremost, thank you to my friend and steadfast writing partner, Jack Martin, whose many suggestions significantly improved these poems. Gratitude also to Bill Tremblay, Alicia Ostriker, and Maggie Anderson.

EYE

For bait they sometimes use pigs' eyes
shoveled from the floor, the slaughter house
windows, eyes painted with blood.

Whose eyes have never been likewise cast down,
pinned fat to stout hooks,
trolled on the junk bottom?

When she fell did she feel the weight roll off?
Did my sister stand over her own mangled body?
Did she skip through the dark like a stone of pure seeing?

Because the candle that burns in the pelvic cradle,
that is an eye.
And so even the blood, and the gasp

and the wheel of the bicycle turning—
spokes fletched with light off hoods of cars—
that is an eye, also.

TORNADO

The distance that surrounds us spreads to let the truck through.
The things you wore, or touched, or loved, thunder by.
All your clothes, and you, living on clouds.
Anyone is anyone.
Heaven feels like far
Even holding breath a long time, everyone breathes.
The intersection you leave is a sound.
Blackbirds rearrange a field.
Bed sheets cross arms on a line.
Moving on is hard.
What if we can't finish the now-what?
You smell like cloves.
Objects float, hardly waiting
to run to you.

I LOOK AT THE APPLE TREE

In the yard, full bloom
like a brain in flower,
magnificent wig, the tree of it,
the upward thrusts, the dip and rise
of thinking,
of singing that happens
on the surfaces opened toward everything—
you and I, the dogs and Isabel—
her apple-flower hand
held to her ear,
Isabel, full of "Hello?"
looking not as we look at this
tree in wonder
(what we can muster)
but at us, or away, her own way—
And the dogs (not) also looking at the fully laden tree
with its limbs in coatings of flowers,
but also at us or away, from the other side
of human language.
Tree of the brain,
pouring out
what the universe pours in:
I take fifty snapshots, hoping to see
what I see.
I picture its other half,
underground, mirror-imaged
roots forming
the hourglass shape of the whole,
sorting the drift in the soil,
the wellings, a smear of rainsoak—
and the flowers
ridden with the bear-shaped
hunger of bees.

BATH

Now with one hand
I brush over Isabel's head,
I sluice the soapy water
from her hair, pouring out
cupfuls I dip. For this sense,
what are right sounds,
as I hold the top of her head,
my hand on the turtle-shell
rattle, the few small beads in it
clicking together her speech,
such as it is: germinal,
nonpredicative, two-
handed.

I know this is how she learns
of herself.
A field sets up in her,
grasps after sounds:
No. Then, yes. Either meaning.
Either meaning, inside this
language ring
she stands. Before her is
yes, then no, then taking
possession.

The children and I were eating chips and drinking iced teas and calculating relative proportions: ant is to tree as person is to X. We assumed ant was one-twelfth of an inch tall, and tree was 112 feet tall. That made tree 16,128 times taller than ant. Too hard to picture. We practiced picturing the ants, twelve of them, standing on each other's backs. We practiced visualizing, holding thumb and first fingers one-twelfth of an inch apart. Twelve ants is unruly, a bizarre tumbling. Horrid! And what tree is 16,128 times taller than us? The children were shrieking from sugar and logic. The three of us average four feet. We poked a calculator on all its buttons. A tree thirteen miles tall, it declared. How tall is that, Caleb asked it. Isabel hid her face in her hands. Is it bigger than the big tree in our yard? he asked her. Do trees keep growing when they're old? he said. Can we have a fire, Daddy?

ANT

You again.
What is it to be you.
Do you walk down
the road or up.
I want to be you
in this way: undistractible.
It would feel good
to speed from the wicker
down a spindle leg
to the separation
opened between
the block foundation
and enfolding earth.
How do you do the dirt,
the ring raised
around your door.

You remind me
of depression,
its climbing swarm
or its trickle,
crossing her smile
to carry her eyes
inside her eyes.
You are mysterious
to us, like serotonin.
Her hand finds mine.
I put sometimes
my head in a closet.
I cannot very well
hold you without
very nearly
doing damage.
Her face is so tired.

What have you found,
down in the cake,
the goodness of the
home ground.
What propels you, wet-looking,
black again, toward the sun.
Ant, show me how
you walk up walls,
step upside-down
on the ceiling.
There is more sky
to be moved
than can be
kept up with.
What she carries
is bigger by as much
as what you carry.
I've seen pictures, ant.
Your tunnels must
thread and join
other tunnels.
What crosses your brain
when you stop,
then what,
when you set forth again?
How much you is in you?

POSTOPERATIVE CARE OF
SMALL WOUNDS

1.

The soul upon leaving the body
must feel sad.
Tactile, like a zipper in search of a garment to close,
the soul must become sustained astonishment.
Undoing the skin, the skin from inside skin,
friendly old breath goes out for—then, what?
Whoa, thinks the soul.
Does regret brim, plumed in five senses?
Dressings must be changed, of course—
sense of touch, sense of smell,
the body bemoans every darkness;
but the soul, like vision, goes on and on,
a tossed morning, fog burned off a coast highway.
Leaving the body, it strands itself, lingers awhile,
milkweed lifting a fence, climbing between wires.
The house behind it, some other home place ahead,
on the stoop it wonders what
it always wondered.

2.

Hurt hand held in his gloved hand,
the surgeon tweezed the loop,
the loop slid down, fastening the wound.
Did I feel pulling, he asked?
The part of that night when my fingers throbbed
I followed the sound of the creek, out the window, as far as I could.
I heard it let itself between rocks, enter and leave the culvert.
Stitches in its sounds; in the stitches, more stitches.

FROM AFAR

My sister's head looks like an apple.
Her beautiful hair is streaming with blood.
Her hands are starfish, flowers gripping pavement.
Everything flows backward from her now:
color on the inside, buds sink into earth.
Her roots return the mineral sky.
Something has tipped. She is falling.
She falls a long time from the end of breathing.
She leaves her body, a traffic light stuck red.
She is not crying. She hears, I swear to God,
the same music when I think of her.
A horse she rides changes direction and form with every stride.
She is what stars carry home to an apple.
From their arsenic purses, the surge of her heat
settles on our shoulders. She is more than flowers.
She glides through our skins like a wave,
lighting it up from inside.

SINGING

Bud keeps yelling about it, but the yellow jackets, scattered broken from the clods by the hooves of the horse, have long flown. Bud keeps yelling how the swarm stood the horses upright. Where he is, is a boy, and the boy in panic watches his sister wing, wide-eyed from the end of the traces. Bud keeps yelling about yellow jackets, keeps pouring carefully around the lawn mower, over the shut lid of the mower's tank, the gasoline he pours as he tells about his sister, singing, gasoline on the ground today, where first one way then back he pulled handsful of moonflowers by the roots. He keeps telling how the yellow jackets swarmed between the horses, how the horses broke, running, how the girl they dragged through the field ended, a voice holding a body held up in a fence. He had a sister who, when he could hear her singing, calmed him. Her voice mixed the sting from the yellow jackets, the hum filling the air like the smell of the moonflowers. He carries armsful in grocery sacks in through the side door. He remembers it sounded like fire running through the air where his sister was singing. In the dark at the end of the driveway, he talks to the light the sun so high in the sky keeps pouring like gasoline onto the ground. He grips and lets go of the wheelbarrow. It is heaped with the stalks and leaves of the moonflowers, landing on him, telling him a name, a name, a name.

STINGRAY

Her bike was coneflower-spoked, a buffalo, a prairie fire combing, the house napped deep in a fold, a pocket of Indian summer. It was night. We slept. My brother. My sisters in their rooms. We slept and slept. Mother, father. Dog. Rabbits in hutches. Goldfish in still, cold water, in a tub dozing at the bottom of the basement stairs. Things slept, hovering. There was her blood. Everywhere, it was friction added to the light. We worked on moving it, morning made visible in spoons, forks, knives. We worked it slow in afternoon with sticks and imagination. Television filled us full of dreams. Our ears set off on training wheels, eyes, shiny pedals. When breath came, enchained with words, it was not her name like flames in chrome plating, like tassels, like ribbons pinned to spokes, but it was how we loved her, never stopped loving her.

PAINTBRUSH LEFT OVERNIGHT
ON THE GROUND ASANA

My wife's yoga teacher talks about sunlight—fire like the sun's—
entering the body through the solar plexus. I picture the cells,
some of them sobbing like old housepainters. "Hey," they start
up. "We're burning daylight." Tiny brushes. Dangling like leaves
in the ash tree's top, rinsed in cold light, the cells shoulder tiny
shadows, carry them, laddering up the walls of the house. Lift-
ing damp tarps in early morning, they whistle, placing the light.
My wife holds our son when he cries. She lets his body practice
remembering her heat, the outline of his foldable self. Sometimes
they sing. The parts they don't know, they fake it.

SUMMER VALLEY

Blown spray from a dogleg waterfall,
the need that comes up
all surfaces, attraction—the falls radiate ions,
they circulate outward, attach the body's own taps
of circulating *chi*—

I've been here all week.
I'm more tired than ever.
I want to fling myself outward.
Every turn leads down more stairways.
I want to know how many languages
intersect here, in this waterfall, its steady rolling.

Helen says later, good idea.
She hasn't a dialectical bone to pick.
Expression and form, she could hardly care less
some emotional drama in whatever subject
is allowed to carry the force.

   Start over:
My sister who is little has grown up inside us.
She is living under water, under the lip
of this flattop granite barn-size boulder
most of which is lodged underground,
a pool here, scooped by the creek.

What happens when light hits the water and the water folds it?

Crest of the falls, swallowtail butterfly.

The old man coming down the basement stairs.

   Start over:
Cleft mountain pouring in, water pouring out.
The bodies of fir trees
shored along the rim, and the one still standing, stripped down.

Metaphor is our first language,
in it we come to the visible trace
of the motion of thought.
Here at the rim of this bowl hollowed out of rock,
the one silvered, wind-beetled fir still standing.

I see: Swallows over the resort opera house,
in light evening wind, flags, dogs turning around and around
not quite able to settle.

   Start over:
My sister who was little has grown up inside.
The mass of Step Mountain catches hold of a color.
My sister is falling under the wheel.
From the newspaper page she moves under water.
Handlebars of the bicycle folded
flat, the run-over frame.

I would trace the form of that gone April evening to say
the things I love. I look for her here in this verging,
swallows *hunting the final curve,*
dogs turning around, standing up, barking.

Downslope drafts sort the warmth from Step Mountain.
Living and not, a deeper breath enters the rooms of the house.
Something invites our attention—all eyes—
and its knowing.

It is dark. I can't see where the next word may fall off the line.
I stand, walk outside in the dark to the phone,
   calling Helen back home in Ohio,
in Ohio, midnight, *time nor space avails not,*
   back home in Ohio where home is,
and dogs barking there also.

POEM FOR A SON

Someone is here, then not.
You know about things from this.
What holds the world, what goes back.
The flower market, its winding, fragrant aisle
passes on to you the hour someone stood,
stock in love, forever in love, grateful loving you.
Now chicory cries blue.
Now tips of the eastern fir trees lift,
a blanket of stars, a mountainside of candles.
Someone is still standing, loving you.
Everyone you know of,
knows from you a flake of this love.
Yes, water whitens its separations.
Yes, atoms slide through the space of other atoms.
Someone here is yet helping you
load your soul on the bus.
Call when you get there,
someone says. And you call.

LULLABY

Among some species of catfish
newly hatched fry
shelter in the mouth of the father.   .

It was in a clear lake
we saw bullheads schooling,
the fry no longer
than a baby's fingers,
the fish, we were told,
shutting them closed
in their mouths at night—
the mouth the whole
of the head, it seemed,
the wafer of brain wedged
between nostrils.

We listened to grown-ups
talking, they held us so;
I want to say we slept
inside their mouths,
grown-ups talking
into the night, children
past their bedtimes, atop
the sound of voices.

I guess this poem
wants to fall asleep also,
inside this figure of
speech it wants to drift,
down in the drowsing
shallows.

And I'm a little sleepy, too.
Thinking of my father as I write,
I try to make him seem
plausibly identical

to the bullhead that dozed
in dock shade.

We might have wiggled
inside him then, a dream
in the roof of his mouth.
We might have crowded
around on his tongue,
our names a stumbling
place in the office
conversation.

If it brought him any pleasure
to say our names out loud
as I do now find pleasure,
ordinary almost, but not quite,
saying the name of my daughter—
if to him some pleasure came
we couldn't know it.

U-PICK ORCHARD

His body fills, touching everything.

*

The trunks loom like atoms. The apples careen between matter and energy, gravity graining the shells.

*

Mounding the trees, the apples ride and plunge.

*

The orchard holds flavors of stars.

*

The crop rivers light like the flowing Ohio. Otter kits streak its currents. The mother quits nursing, dives. Knifing the cold, she stings a fish in her teeth.

*

The orchard man says to everyone the same: "Walk to the Y, go left then right." Heads high, we walk. We pick halfway from the row end. Our sacks bulge, weighing us down. We spread out, the grass in the Y warming our feet. Apples thump, falling all over. The ground goes slow, eating.

*

To feel the river, deer come.

*

At the Y worn into the orchard grass, three women stand, hands on their pregnant bellies. They learn by touch the bulge of elbow, plinth of knee.

*

Phoenician incense, amphorae of myrrh sail the blue.

*

Boxes set in rows, made rosy almost evenly by the falling light, hold biblical numbers of bees.

*

The women bend into the weight of the branches, shallowly breathing. More brightly as the day shortens, they pause; they glow like paper lanterns with what empties through them, lighting a trail.

*

Our son in the Y of his mother's legs remembers that road and runs. Around and around, he could have been anyone's, he chases everything. Can we not see? "Look how fast," he calls. "Watch me!"

*

Our daughter looks up, looks around, watching.

*

We are four mouths, four tongues, four stomachs moaning in honey. We are eight eyes, eight ears, eight hands. Our noses bring the place we almost feel. The deepest bliss, tucked like a star inside our heads, summer winds its flesh to a stem. We are combed with humming.

*

Our bed, the grass. Fingers come into our mouths, sweet with pickings.

MEMORIAL FOR MY LIFE

This last week on earth, I should have written more.
I had a story. A world coming to blossom.
Passing over birthdays, death days, on and on it came,
and I almost got it, the way it
folded outward, a blossom.
First, it was wind.
At night when no one can see rain falling,
it was rain falling.
The weightlessness of my story sponged me upward.
Among weightless leaves, I heard it tread.
From the depths of trees it popped, it was nothing.
For a time I caressed it, tender as my newborn's ear,
discovering in it, its hidden
curves and softness, as of the new oak leaf.
I should have.
Written more.
Goddam.
Without finishing, someone now will brighten the room with lights.
He or she will turn, weakened by my crying—
deep in my death, my afterlife forever, a surface barely scratched.
My baby turns into an owl chick.
The owl returns to towering woods.
In that place, a tire swing hangs on like everything.
Over the worn track,
my baby's feet skim back and forth. From under the ground
my smile grows.
There was listening, someone explains.
There was what was.
Come back where you come back. Your life looked like this
from outside.

WHAT MY PARENTS DID

She was rain and hailstones, but him I couldn't see. He was over the horizon whirling things up, meeting his destructive down-blast. She, I could see turn, face reddened over the skillet, eyes pooling. He, I could feel, the slight change lowering pressure, the closeness attending the gathering storm, the before and after.

She was present where he hid, a fold of air too heavy to breathe. He was thunder traveling its quietest edge, barely audible. She was lightning, broken flashes rearranging the night, trees in a flurry of bending suddenly exposed.

He was red lights and silos, what radar detected forming in clouds. The next county up he was hours of watch. She was rain flooding down, the creek, blown out of its banks. He was smoke from blown transformers, the woods powdered with ozone smell.

She was the dark with the lights knocked out, all the lines down. He was calling but she couldn't hear. He was lifting her with his breath and she was hardly there. He was blowing the house sideways to save us.

WHAT THE DEAD DON'T DO

Is care what time it is,
how long you stay, how near or far
from the lip of their specific crumbly grave?
You are the last thing they're dreaming.
They don't think about music,
nor the earrings nor the flavor of the soda
you shared; how sticky the glass.
News pages crawl in the feet of some wind.
Through the whispering grass—
the dead don't read all about it.
They don't act like a girl.
They don't sneak a taste. At the party, playing
hostess, they don't cruise around,
dip squares of icing and cake to each plate.
Plunged like tongues struck dumb in the ground,
they don't glad-hand back through the welcome ring,
don't blush and mingle,
the bottomless well of their sexy bodies
filling the spigots with whoosh.
Who's there? some call, peering deep.
No one starts up the long blank hole,
or swims from the black car's back door.
No one stands, sounding the doorbell chimes.

X

My sister who lives in heaven visited last night. She walked figure eights in the living room, dragging a hobbyhorse stick. Her hair was shorter, a surfer girl's. She had a story and, man, she told it. About algebra, and the shape of infinity. Barefoot, she walked to a mountain classroom: math, college. "¾ divided by ½ = X" she wrote on the board. "Look at the X. Where did it come from? Whoever invented X was a genius." Out the door, she pointed to the end of the driveway: morning, a paper in a sheer wrapper folded; the sky attaching by the slender bright edge, the hidden face of the moon.

BIRDS FLY

O, child, they do.
There never is a final word.
No last lesson for the clan.
Beyond rain, beyond windrow,
they do not stop.
In the march of the sun, they go and go.
One day from one hill when we watch,
the tiny spirals bury the hawks in the sky.
Everything is where we saw it,
only deeper after that.
Birds fly, child.
All night they do not stop.
They go where they are going.
And so you do.
And so do I.

NOTES

"Summer Valley": *metaphor . . . the motion of thought* is adapted from Suzanne Langer; *time nor space avails not* comes from Walt Whitman; and *hunting the final curve* comes from William Stafford.